I0532658

ORCHIDS CRYING IN HEAVY RAIN

POETRY

ANGELO SPIZZARRI

Book page layout and cover design by Angelo Spizzarri

PRINTED IN THE UNITED STATES OF AMERICA
THIS BOOK IS PRINTED ON ACID FREE PAPER

ISBN 979-8-9869000-0-1

All words, face logo & cover art by: Angelo Spizzarri

WE CAN
DESTROY
OURSELVES
BETTER THAN
ANYONE ELSE

CONTENTS

1 THE GAUZE THE FILTER
2 CHAOS
3 SPECTRAL
4 SEEKING
5 CHAINS
6 SEASHORE
7 VENTRICLE
8 LOTUS LEAF
9 BLACK BROKEN TEETH
10 SWANS WON'T REMEMBER
11 FEAR
12 CRUSHED IN DISGUISE
13 SEVEN TONGUES OF FLAME
14 IN YOUR HANDS
15 NO LONGER NEEDED
16 WEAVE MEMORY VEINS
17 ASHES WHITE AS SNOW
18 VIRUS
19 WOMB SO HELPLESS
20 THE TORSO
21 NEURON
22 STORM
23 THE BRIDGE
24 MEMORY
25 MELTING TOWER
26 TREE AND ABSENCE OF CHRONOS
27 BLOODSTREAM
28 SALT TEARS
29 FLATLINE
30 RED SEA
31 A PROMISE
32 TUNNEL VISION
33 THE HOLY ONE
34 MESSIAH

35 SKIN OF THE CRYING TREE
36 THE GOLDEN EMBRYO
37 LEECH
38 GLASS TONGUE
39 QUARANTINED
40 MALIGNANCY
41 PAST TENSE
42 MEMORY DUST
43 EMPTINESS
44 FORBIDDEN LOW FEVER
45 LETHARGY WASTED
46 WRAITH CRIES IN WAVES
47 DETERIORATE LIKE MEMORY
48 SUFFER THE ISLAND TWIN
49 FLESH STOLEN BUT NOT OBTAINED
50 PROTECTION WILL BURN
51 CREMATORIUM
52 HUNGER
53 TEARS OF THE POPPY
54 SIGHT OF THE REDEEMER
55 MECHANISM
56 THE PAST
57 CLOCK
58 SCREAM WANTED RELEASE
59 YESTERDAY
60 INNER DEATH
61 SOLILOQUY
62 LOST STAR
63 SYNTHESIS
64 LEAF BEGAN TO DIE ONCE
65 RIP AT YOUR CHEST
66 THE SCREAMING LOTUS
67 PANDEMONIUM
68 UGLY

CONTENTS CONTINUED

69 SOFT LIQUID CRY
70 THE STRANGE SUN IS GONE
71 TRANSITION OF SOUL
72 FROM THE MUTE VISION
73 INJECTOR
74 WEAVE MOIST SKIN
75 UNLOCK
76 WAKE THE SHAKES
77 THIN MIND
78 CHROME TEETH LIQUID NAILS
79 I MAKE LOVE
80 I DON'T WANT YOU HERE
81 MY NUMB HEART
82 BLACK WRAPPED FLESH
83 I LOVED ONCE
84 MOONBEAM TRANSPARENT
85 TEARDROP MEMORY
86 SENSATION
87 FIRE BURNING AWAY
88 I ACHE FOR
89 WHY SHOULD
90 IF SCARS
91 THOUGHT
92 MERCURIAL STARS
93 SEA SALT DROWNED
94 THE SUN IS GONE
95 STARS ABOVE
96 BRAIN DEAD
97 FEAR RUSHING INTO
98 I KEPT IT FOR
99 INDIGO BLOSSOMS
100 SLEEPWALKING

ORCHIDS CRYING
IN HEAVY RAIN

POETRY

ANGELO SPIZZARRI

THE GAUZE THE FILTER

RELAX FLOAT ON DOWN
TO NEVER THOUGHT
EAT AWAY THE MIND OF BEING
SURRENDER YOUR
TONGUE TO THE RAZOR
NO WORDS ARE NEEDED
LAY INTO THE GAUZE
TO FILTER OUT
THE BLACK GEMINI
INSIDE YOUR EYE
THAT LOOKS AT NOT INTO
TO FIND AN END
TO SPEAKING
REACH IN AND
TURN IT INSIDE OUT
SO BACKWARDS NOW
THE SCREAM THAT HARMS
WILL SING ME TO SLEEP

A BUTTERFLIES DREAM

CHAOS

I AM LOST
HEAVY HEART
AT THE CENTER
WAILING ENDLESS
DISTANT STAR IN THE
SKY FOREVER BURNING
MANTIS WAITS IN EONS
FOR REALIZATION
BLOSSOM FALLING
FROM ORGASM SKIES
DO NOT FEAR ONE DAY
IT WILL COME SOON
UNPREDICTABLE
AS THE SUN AND
HEAVY AS A TEAR
IN THE NUCLEAR BOMB

SPECTRAL

REFLECTIONS
OF THE MOON
RIPPLES ON THE
SURFACE OF SEA
MORPHOSES THE
CRESCENT INTO
A SPECTRAL
ECLIPSED PEARL
EXPLODING LIKE THE
DOUBLE NOVA CORONA
DANCING FOR
EYES OF NO ONE
EXCITED THRASHING
REFRACTED DANCING
FLUORSECENT BEAUTY
SENSUAL WAVES
OF THE STARS ECHO
STOP MOTIONS RIPPLES
DISAPPEAR TO SLEEP

SEEKING

SEEKING THE WRONG THING
ALWAYS SEEING IT BEFORE I ACT
IT'S STILL THE WRONG THING
CONFUSED I REMEMBER HOW
IT IMPACTED MY LIFE IN NEGATION
MANY TIMES BUT YET STILL
ALWAYS SEEKING THE SAME
BEHAVIOR PATTERN
USING DIFFERENT THINGS
DIPPING MY FINGERS IN CEMENT
BUT WHEN IT DRIES
WHAT DO I DO THEN?

CHAINS

NEARER THE SUNRISE
FLESH HOT WITH FEVER
SWALLOW IN MY
THROAT HURTS
METAL FLAKES
PEELING ITCHING SKIN
THESE CHAINS
SO HEAVY COLD
FURIOUS THEY
KEEP ME DRAINED
SITTING IN A BALL
ON CONCRETE FLOOR
CRUSHED FROM
A HOLLOW WEIGHT
MIND SILENT NOTHING
BUT NUMB LINE HUNGRY
FOR INSANITY
LONELY FOR ANYONE
CONSTRICTION OF LINKS
UPON MY MEMORY
FURTHER THE SUNSET

SEASHORE

ONE MOTION CHRONOS
SKIES WERE GRAYSCALE
BARELY BREATHING BRUISED
LOVE WASHED UP UPON
THE SEASHORE OF TEARS
AS MOTION REVOLVED LOVE
BECAME COVERED
WITH SKIN CELL
IT SHOOK AND SHIVERED
COLD HUNGRY LONELY
IT WOKE FROM NEAR
DROWNING MEMORY OF
SALIVA AND LOCKJAW
CHRONOS AURA BEAM
OF ANAESTHESIA
HIT LOVE WHERE
IT LAID IN WASTE
THIS TIME IT WOULD
HAVE TO RETURN LOVE
ONCE AGAIN TO THE
LAND OF THE LIVING
AND NUMB

VENTRICLE

UPON MOTIONS FOUND
THE FLESH OF HEART
ITS MALFUNCTION WAS
DISCOVERED WITHIN
A HEART WAS TORN
ONE OF THE TWO
CHAMBERS RUPTURED
FROM SURIGICAL
STEEL INCISION
OF ACUTE DEPRESSION
SPECTRE CAME TO FIND
THIS SERIOUS
CONDITION INOPERABLE
THE ONLY THING
IT COULD DO WAS
FEED THIS PATIENT
CONCENTRATED
MEMORIES OF THE PAST
ALTHOUGH HOPELESS
SPECTRE WONDERED
WILL THIS HEART
EVER BEAT AGAIN

LOTUS LEAF

OXYGEN AIR FEELS LIKE
NEEDLES OF GLASS FROM
INDIGO ATMOSPHERE
WHERE LOTUS LEAF LAID
TORN IN THE RAIN
ITS COLOR WAS
SHOCK WHITE
WIND RUSHED
THROUGH A TEAR
CAUSING HURT
TO THE BLOSSOM
THAT WAS MISSING THIS
PIECE REMAINED WHEN
THE LOTUS FLOWER
FIRST OPENED UP
TO THE VERSE OF UNI
BUT OH HOW COULD THIS
HAVE BEEN LEFT BEHIND
STILL THE WIND RUSHED
FORCING VERTICAL GLASS
TO FALL FROM AIR
NO CONTROL
THE BLOSSOM
NO WHERE

BLACK BROKEN TEETH

TEETH GNASHING ON
THAWED BLEACHED
PERVERSE SENSES
SHAKY AS BONE
COMES DOWN
DEVOURING THEM
ONE BY ONE
TO SATISFY THE
ITCHING OF SOMETHING
DEEPER THAN HUNGER
TO FEED A VEIN
AND MIND BLOOD
TEARING TO SEVER
THE ANGER CONSTRAINT
WHEN ONE DOESN'T
SEE ANYTHING WRONG
WITH ONES BEHAVIOR THEN
THERE IS NO REASON
TO CHANGE IT
FRACTURE A FEW TEETH
BUT KEEP CHEWING

SWANS WON'T REMEMBER

COLLIDING STARS IN THE
OILY VERSE OF UNI
DRIFT LIKE SLIPSTREAM
MATTER WITH ANTI – GRAVITY
RIPPLING RINGS OF STARDUST
THE SWANS ONE BY ONE
SWIM SLOWLY ACROSS
UNI – VISION OF NEBULA GAS
THEY STRETCH WINGS OUT
SEEMING TO REACH
OF EDGE OF GALAXY
UPON GAZING THEY
SWIM A VACUUM DANCE
TO WHERE ONE KNOWS NOT
SWANS WON'T REMEMBER YOU
FROM 3 – DIMINSIONAL DREAMS
IT IS NOT FOR YOU TO CONTROL
WHAT YOU NEVER
HAD NO CONTROL OF

FEAR
REACHING

FEAR
REACHING
ORGASM
WITHOUT
CRAVING
A GHOST
FAR AWAY
IS WEEPING

CRUSHED IN DISGUISE

MY SOUL IS SLICED
MANY SECTORS EACH
A PRISONER OF
THE MIND PRISON
REJECTION SCREAMING
NERVE ENDINGS
HALLUCINATE
WITHIN PRESSING
GLASS WALLS
NOTHING EXISTS
URGES OF ABORTION OF
UN – EMOTION AND ANXIETY
KILL AND CRUSH ME
IN EVERY EMPTY MOMENT
OF THIS WOMB
WHERE IN DISGUISE
ONE EXISTS EVEN
PAIN ISN'T ACCEPTED
IN A NON – DREAM STATE
ONE LEARNS TO HIDE
AND DIE INSIDE

SEVEN TONGUES
OF FLAME

SHOUTING VIBRATIONS
ATTACKED LIKE FLAME
WHITE ORANGE RED
BURNING MORE THAN FLESH
HEAVY MORE THAN BLACK HOLE
ATTACKING THEY ALWAYS DO
AMBUSH NEVER EXPECTED
JUDGEMENT OF THE
SEVEN FORMS OF SIN
ACID ON THE BODY
IT COMES IN MANY FORMS
IN ALL DIRECTIONS
EVEN IN SLEEP
THE MIND AND MEMORY
NEVER FORGET
DREAMS REVISIT
AND REPLAY
THE DAMAGE OF
HURTING IN FLAME

IN YOUR HANDS

HEART AN
UN – EXPECTED PRISON
LOVE THE
UN – AWARE VICTIM
WHEN LOVE IS FOUND
ONE TRIES WITH
EVERY ATOM
OF EXISTENCE
TO HOLD ONTO
THIS ESSENCE
ENTER LOVE IT DIES
WITH A CRY IN HANDS
THAT HOLD IT CAPTIVE
WITH NO SUSTENANCE
CAN KILL EVEN WHEN
INNOCENT INTENTION
IS APPARENT BUT
WHEN SUFFOCATION
EXTERMINATES
ONE EVERY NAIL
IS FELT ON FLESH
WHERE LIVING ONE
CAN APPEAR DEAD

NO LONGER NEEDED

A FLESH BEING LIES
IN UN – DIMENSION WHERE
SILENCE SCREAMS
LIKE THUNDER
LIQUIDS DRAIN
AND SKIN DECAYS
IN JAGGED FAST
MOTION FRAME
NOW THE RIB CAGE
EXPOSED EMPTY
PEACOCKS LAND FROM
VACUUM AND DANCE
AROUND THE CORPSE
CELEBRATION
IN MUTED LIGHT
EGO IN THE BEING WAS
NO LONGER NEEDED
FOR ONCE THE
PATH NIRVANA
HAS BEEN FOUND
SOUL HAS NO NEED FOR
FLESH BLOOD OR
NEGATED DEFECT
OF BEHAVIOR
PATTERN

WEAVE MEMORY VEINS

INTO THE BRAIN WIRE
VEINS EXPLODE OUT
FROM THIS SKULL
SEARCHING
THEY SMELL FOR
EXTREMITIES
WRAP AROUND
LIMBS AND FEED
OUTSIDE IN FROM MANY
NEURO TANSMITTERS
RECEIVING
IMAGO LINGO
FORMULAE
VIA THE LIQUID DREAM
OF SALINE SEED
FIND THE PSEUDO
SELF THAT BETRAYED
THE SKIN WRAPPED
SELF BY END CYCLE
ONE WILL UNDERSTAND
WHY BUT IN SILENCE
THE SEED WILL SIGH

ASHES WHITE AS SNOW

A CITY DEAD GRAY
EMPTY OF LIVING ENTITIES
SLEEPS IN ISLOATION
THE HEAVY CLOUDS FLOAT LOW
SCRATCH SCRAPPING THE
TOWERING SKY SCRAPERS
FALLING LIKE SNOW ASH DRIFTS
SLOW MOTION DOWN TO WHERE
THE LAST BEATING ESSENCE LAYS
BLOODY BLEEDING FROM
A WAR WAGED WITHIN ITSELF
THE WAR FOUGHT AND LOST
NOTHING REMAINS OF
WHAT WAS AND WHAT IS NOW
GENTLE BREEZE TOUCHED THE
FRAGILE BEING CARESSING IT
UNTIL THE LAST VEIN PUMPED
FUNCTION WAS ALL LOST

VIRUS

FIRST STAGE
INJECTED
DIS – EASE OF SELF
LEECHES ONTO
WHITE BLOOD CELL
SUCKING LIFE
OUT SMALL PARTS
BEGINS TO
REPLICATE ITSELF
SECOND STAGE
GEOMETRICALLY
DIS – EASE GROWS
RAPIDLY UNTIL
CELL MUTILATION
BEGINS RAGE INITIATION
INVASION ACHIEVED
THIRD STAGE
FLESH MALFUNCTIONS
THOUGHT PROCESS
SHAKES HALT
LIFEFORCE SHOCKED
DEATH IMMINENT
RAGE CRIES
BODY DIES

WOMB SO
HELPLESS

ELASTIC SKIN
SAC SCREAMING
UNCONTROLLED
DEEP QUAKES
THAT PUNCH
UTERINE WALLS
HANDS THAT
CLAW AND TEAR
AT NIGHTMARE
OF FETUS TRUMA
BARRIER STRETCHED
MEMBRANE STRAIN
BONE AND MUSCLE
BARING UN – LIFE
IT DOES NOT EXIST
UNTIL FREE OF THIS
BRITH CANAL
DON'T ESCAPE YOUR
CONFORT ZONE
THIS VIOLENT WORLD
IS TOO MUCH

THE TORSO

TORSO SEPARATED
BY LIQUID SPACE
SLICED BY BROKEN NERVE
AND CRYING TEARS
THAT CANNOT BE
CONTROLLED BY ITSELF
DIPPED WITHIN AN INKY PLACE
OF HIDDEN SECRETS
FLUID FLESH THE SAME
SOILED GHOST WHICH
IS CONTROLLED BY
THE CRYING TEARS
OF ACHING SEPARATION
A REVERSE BIRTH OF
A SECRET THAT
SHOULDN'T EVEN
EXIST

NEURON

ON THE OCEANS EDGE
WAVES OF MOON DUST
ROLLS WITH NO GRAVITY
QUADRAPED HUMANOIDS
DANCED WITH BLANK FACE
SOME HELD INSECT NETS
TO CAPTURE MOTHS WITH
FLUORESCENT SKIN
AS THE RED PLANETOID
HUNG ABOVE ITS
RIPPLING IMAGE UPON
MOONS DUST EDGED HORIZON
RUNNING INVERTED CHRONOS
MOTION OF OCEAN WAVE
ALL WAS A FLEETING MOMENT
THAT HAD LIFE AS LONG AS
THE NEURON ELECTRIC
FLICKER DREAM

STORM

UPON SILENT SEA
UP INTO THE CLOUDS
CELLOPHANE ANGELS
FLEW DOWN FROM
WHITE BLUE HEAVENS
WHIRLING AND SKATING
ACROSS THE SURFACE
OF WATER THEY BEGAN
TWISTING AND TURNING
UNTIL A BLUR OF WIND
COULD ONLY BE SEEN
AS THE CLOUDS FUSED
IN GRAYSCALE
THE SUN LEFT AND
THE SEA STORM FELL
FROM THE SKIES
A TRANQUIL SCENE
OF SYNERGY

THE BRIDGE

BEYOND THE FADED GREEN DISTANCE
STOOD STAIRS DISINTEGRATING AND
THE BRIDGE THAT ENDED IN MID AIR
WHERE THE WINGED ONES CAME TO
SEE IF THEY COULD RETURN FLY BACK
TO THE SHIMMER CITY IN ITS HIDDEN
4TH – DIMENSION AS ONE BY ONE
EACH WAITED AND THEN BEGAN LEAPING
OFF SOME FLEW STRONG AND SWIFT
WHILE OTHERS JUMPED TO THEIR DEATH
OR PURGATORIES FOR MANY DIED
THAT DAY FOR THEY HAD NO DESIRE TO
REALLY RETURN BUT THE ONES THAT
DID HAD TO LET GO OF THE PAST
WHERE THEY ROSE UP TO WHERE THEY
SO WANTED TO RETURN NEVER
GAZING BACK INTO THE PAST

MEMORY

SPECTRE SURFACED ON AFARS EDGE
HORIZON PALE YELLOW SUN BEHIND
MAKING HIM AND MOUNTAIN BLACK
LIVING SHADOWS FOR HE COULD NOT
HARNESS THE FEELING OF TIME
FOR HIS FLESH WAS A MERE MEMORY
DISINTEGRATED JUST A GHOST LOST
WANDERING LOST IN A STATIC PLACE
HE CAN NOT FEEL SEARCHING FOR
A SELF THAT HE CAN NOT REMEMBER
NOT KNOWING WHERE HE HAS BEEN
WHERE HE IS GOING OR WHY HE JUST
REALIZED ALL THIS WAS LIKE A FADED
MEMORY HIS SENSE VEIN JUST
COULDN'T HOLD ONTO ANYMORE

MELTING TOWER

INSIDE ITS COCOON OF MANTA STARS
THE MELTING TOWER STOOD UPON
A LONE ROCK A VICTIM OF THE WAVES
WALLS CEILINGS SAGGED AND BEND
STAIRCASE MORPHED TO DOWNWARDS
SPIRAL ITS MAIN BODY TWISTING OVER
LIQUID SHAPESHIFT LEANING SLOWLY
LIKE HEATED WAX IN A BURSTING SUN
WORLD IT WAS NOT STRONG ENOUGH
TO WITHSTAND THE CRUSHING BEATING
WAVES ON ITSELF OVER AND OVER AND
DEFEAT OF THE COCOON CAME OF
ITS OWN TEARS THAT WERE USED TO
DROWN ITSELF INTO ICE COLD OCEAN
WHERE THE ROCK IS ALL THAT REMAINED

TREE AND ABSENCE
OF CHRONOS

IN A LAND SPACE FORGOT STOOD
HIDDEN A TREE WORN GNARLED
ABUSED BY CHRONOS BUT UPON
CLOSER INSPECTION ITS BODY
RESEMBLED HUMAN TORSO AND
LIMBS AS THE DARK WIND BLOWS
FROM THE EAST OF ORIFICES
UNKNOWN THE GALE GUSTS HURT
AGAINST HER HARDENED SKIN
FOR SHE NEVER WANTED TO CHANGE
THE STUBBORN ANGER AND THE
INSISTANCE OF HER DEFECTS KEPT HER
HARD AND RIGID SO ONCE CHRONOS
HAD CLAIMED THE SANDS OF HER
HOURGLASS THIS WAS NOW HER
FINAL PLACE OF REST CAUSE ONCE
TIME HAS BEEN TAKEN NOTHING CAN
EVER BE CHANGED SO AS IN LIFE ONE
WILL EXIST IN A DIMENSION OF ONES
OWN FINAL DEFECTS AND CHOICES

BLOODSTREAM

I TOUCH YOUR HEART
IN THIS STILLNESS
THROUGH ITS CHEST
WHERE EMOTION CAN
ABSORB INTO MY
BLOOD STREAM
SO THIS HEART CAN
VISIT MINE AGAIN AND AGAIN
IF THIS COULD ONLY LAST
WAIT ONLY A LITTLE
WHILE LONGER
SO I DON'T FORGET
ITS SENSATION
SO I WILL KNOW IT AGAIN
WHEN IT FINDS ME
A GRAIN OF SAND
IN THIS MASSIVE EXISTENCE

SALT TEARS

TENDER KISS OF
THIS TEAR DROP
ITS SALT LIKE TONGUE
WRAPS AROUND MY GHOST
IN THE SILENT GARDEN
OF SPLINTERED GLASS
SHIMMERING IN
LIQUID ISOLATION
A LIVING WRITHING THING
THAT COMFORTS ME
FOR WHEN I'M INSIDE
MY COCOON CHOKING
I HAVE THESE SALT TEARS
TO KEEP ME SAFE

FLATLINE

A BED IS HERE EMPTY
THE WHITE SHEET FULL OF DUST
FORMS THE OUTLINE OF WHERE
THE BODY OF SADNESS USED TO LIE
SO HEAVY WAS THE WEIGHT
SO WET WERE THOSE TEARS
SO DEAD WAS THE SOUL
THAT LAID HERE FOR
FAR TOO LONG THAT THIS
IMPRINT WAS ALL THAT REMAINS
OF THE MEMORY OF THE
SADNESS THAT LIVED AND DIED
A LIFE OF FLATLINE

RED SEA

RED SEA CHURNING
SWRILING RAGE BURNING
BLOOD VESSEL ACHES
FOR THE RAZORS REALITY
TO BRING REBIRTH OF DESIRE
TO RAISE ONE UP FROM
THIS BED OF NAILS
NEW AND GLEAMING
WITH ITS OWN EUPHORIA
THAT PUMPS INTRAVENOUS
CONFLICTION IN FORMS FOR
FORGOTTEN SALIVATING DREAMS
WANTING OBLIVION BUT ONE
TOO AFRAID TO CHASE AFTER IT

A PROMISE

THE LAST DAY TO KNOW MYSELF
THE LOST SOULS KEEP A PROMISE
TO KNOW MY KARMA AND
IGNITE THE LIFEFORCE ECHOES
SO FRAGILE AND DELICATE
AS THE JELLYFISH FLOATING
IN THE SEA OF VERSE OF UNI
RELAXING WITHOUT SPEAKING
BEYOND FEELING A PEACE OF SELF
GOING TO SELF BACK INTO SELF
CLEAN FROM STAINS LONG AGO
FROM BEING A LIVING BREATHING
HUMAN CAN LEAVE BEHIND

TUNNEL VISION

AN OCEAN CHURNS IN OSMOSIS
THE SKY WHITE AS SCAR FLAME
2 – DIMENSIONAL MOUTH SUSPENDED
AT THE CORE THE BLIND ONE CAME
SPITTED FORTH FROM ITS LIPS AS IF
WET BIRTH SLICK BODY CRASHING
INTO THE COLD WAVES WHEN THE
BLIND ONE SURFACED HE GAZED
SHOCKED UP AT THIS STERN MOUTH
ABOVE HIM SAID NOTHING BUT STARED
DOWN AT HIM GLARING TUNNEL VISION
HAD BEEN A DISEASE IN HIS MIND MATTER
SO SELF ABSORBED HIS THOUGHTS HIS
VERY BEING AND THEN THE MOUTH
HANGING OVER THE OCEAN WAS JUDGE
OVER NEGATION AND SENTENCED
THE BLIND ONE TO BE ABSORBED INTO
THIS OCEAN AS HE ALLOWED SELF
CENTEREDNESS TO ABSORB WITHIN HIM

THE HOLY ONE

INSIDE THIS CRACK IN THE MATTER OF
CONTINUUM THE GOLDEN CITY SHONE
AS BRIGHT AS THE SURFACE OF SUN
FAR FROM REACH FROM INFLUENCE
MURMURS OF THE HOLY ARE HEARD
EVERYWHERE ENTRANCING THE MANY
WALK ALL OVER IN SILENCE FOR PRAISE
BE TO THE HOLY ONE THEY ALL LIVE FOR
THEIR IRREVERSIBLE CHOICE BEHOLD
THE CENTER OF THE CITY HERE HE IS
BODYLESS BUT FOR A FLESHLESS VEIN
COVERED MIND MATTER ENCASED IN
MINERAL CRYSTAL FLOATING ETERNAL
NON – GRAVITY AND BEHIND THE SUICIDE
TREE BARING FRUIT ONE CANNOT EAT
UNLESS ONE INVITES REBIRTH FOR THE
HOLY ONE CANNOT SPEAK BUT AS ONE
KNEELS TO HIM AND PRAYS OPENING
ONES MIND THE HOLY ONE EMITS QUAKE
VIBRATION IN PULSE RHYTHM AND THE
ANSWER COMES IN STRETCHED CHRONOS
YES HE CANNOT SPEAK BUT HE WAITS FOR
EACH ONE TO FIND THEIR OWN INNER VOICE
AND FREE THEMSELVES FROM THE MURMURS
DISTRACTION OF THE MANY TO BECOME ONE

MESSIAH

ANOINTED ONE STOOD ON THE EDGE
OF THE 4TH – DIMENSION HE SEES HIS
PEOPLE OF 100 FOLLOWERS THEY
WAITED AND HE SPOKE OF HOW THE
TIME HAD COME FOR THE UNI – FICATION
OF THE SELF AND WHERE HIS PEOPLE
READY AND THEY WERE AND THE ANOINTED
ONE ANNOUNCES THE BIRTH OF THE
FETUS PERFECTION TO ENTER THIS
DIMENSION AND LEAD US TO A NEW
NIRVANA THAT EXISTS BUT IS UNKNOWN
AND AS THIS PRE – DETERMINED EVENT
HAPPENS AND LO THE FETUS PERFECTION
IS BIRTHED FROM GELATIN LIGHT FLOATING
FREE THE FOLLOWERS IN AWE GIVE THEIR
LIVES UP TO THIS PERFECTION AS ONE BY ONE
EACH OF THIS FLOCK WHISPERS ITS SIN TO
THIS FETUS IT OPENS ITS MOUTH AND
CONSUMES THEM ONE BY ONE ONCE ALL ARE
GONE TO THEIR NEW PROMISED NIRVANA
THE ANOINTED ONE SAYS TO THE FETUS
NO I WILL NOT BE JOINING YOU FOR UNLIKE
THEM I DO NOT BELIEVE IN THIS FALSE PLACE
JUST BECAUSE THEY DID THEN ANOINTED ONE
SLOWLY TURNED AND BEGAN HIS RETURN
FROM THE EDGE OF THIS 4TH – DIMENSION

SKIN OF THE CRYING TREE

INSIDE THE CLOUD OF STORM STOOD
A PLACE WHERE A TRAIL OF THIN LEAF
SKINS LITTERED ALL OVER AND AS ONE
FOLLOWED THE TRAIL IT LEAD TO THE
CRYING TREE IT WAS VERY OLD GNARLED
WHITE GRAY LIKE THE CLOUD ITSELF
AND AT THE BASE NAKED ROOTS LARGE
AND SMALL PILES OF STRIPS OF THIS DRIED
PAPERLIKE FLESH LAID ALL AROUND EACH
SNAKE LIKE SKIN WAS A LOVE TAKEN AWAY
OR THAT JUST SIMPLY DIED AWAY MILLIONS
BLEW AND SCATTERED AROUND THIS PLACE
OCCASSIONALLY BIRDS WOULD FLY IN WITH
A BEAUTIFUL SONG EACH COMPLETELY UNIQUE
TO EACH BIRD FILLING IT AND THEN LEAVING
THE INDIGO RED ROSE AMBER SUN BEGINS TO
SET FOR ANOTHER NIGHT FOR THE CRYING TREE
IS ALWAYS AWAKE NO SLEEP CAN CURE IT
AND ALL THROUGH THE DUSK AND NIGHT
AS THE SKIN LEAVES BLOW AND CREATES
THE SOUND OF HUSHED CRIES AND DISTANT SIGHS
SONATA OF EACH BIRD SINGS INSIDE ITS SIGHS

THE GOLDEN EMBRYO

IN THE BEGINNING BEING CAME INTO
CHRONOS WHERE KALEIDOSCOPIC
OCEANS OF GAS ATMOSPHERE SWIRLING
STOOD A LARGE GLASS CYLINDER TUBE
IT ROSE UP FROM PLUMES AND SMOKE
LIKE FINGER WAVES ONE LIFE FORCE
FLOATED UPWARDS INSIDE THE TUBE
THE GOLDEN EMBRYO HAD ARRIVED
CELESTIAL OBLATION WAS NEEDED BUT
WHO WOULD CARRY THIS OUT FOR THE
EMBRYO NEEDED AN ORGAN INTERNAL
HEALED INSIDE MOMENTS PASSED ON
THEN HUMAN FLESH CELL WITH BLANK
FACE CAME AND FOUND ITSELF AT THIS
MONOLITHIC VICINITY FLOATED OVER
ASKED A QUESTION IT WAS ANSWERED
THEN BLANK FACE USED FINGERNAIL
TO CUT ITS FLESH REMOVING THE SKIN
ON ITS ARMS LEGS LASTLY ITS FACE TO
FORM A BLOOD CLOT FROM HIS FLESH
BLANK FACE OFFERED UP THIS OBLATION
WITH COMPLETE DEVOTION AND THUS
GOLDEN EMBRYO GRANTED A GIFT FOR
THE SKINLESS ONE THAT WOULD GAIN
ENTRY INTO NEXT LIFE AS THE EMBRYO
SEWED UP ITS NEW HEART BLINKED ITS
EYES SOON SKINLESS ONE VAPORIZED
INTO THE ATOMLESS TO LIVE ANOTHER
FORM IN ANOTHER AFTER WORLD LIMBO

LEECH

SAND DUNES AND YELLOW DIRT DUST
CRACKED DYING LAY FOREVER IN ALL
DIRECTIONS DISTANT MOUNTAINS SIT
IN HAZY YELLOW DUST AS IF CRYING
FOR NEED LEECH HUNCHED WALKED
IN CREEPING STANCE SOMETHING HE
SPOTTED SEEMED OUT OF PLACE HERE
THEN BEFORE HIM WAS AN APPERATUS
OF UNKNOWN ORIGIN THERE WERE 2
HYPO – NEEDLES ON 2 TABLES ATTACHED
TO 2 TANKS AND 2 CHAIRS ONE INVITED
THE OTHER DIDN'T LEECH WANTED WHAT
WAS HOOKED INTO THE TANKS FOR MORE
WAS NEVER ENOUGH BUT WHICH ONE
LEECH SAT AT THE ONE THAT INVITED
SAT DOWN AND DROVE THE STEEL SPIKE
INTO HIS VEIN AS THE MACHINE SPRUNG
TO LIFE AND HE SAT THERE WAITING
FOR HIS EUPHORA BUT AFTER MOMENTS
NONE CAME THEN NOTICED HE WAS
FEELING WEAK BUT STILL WAITED THEN
SAW HIS ARM WAS SHRINKING SLOWLY
AND FEAR BEGAN AS PANIC LEECH
TRIED TO REMOVE THE HYPO BUT HE
WAS INTENSELY EXHAUSTED AS THE
APPERATUS WAS SUCKING OUT HIS LIFE
LIKE LEECH USED TO SUCK MORE FROM
EVERYTHING WHEN AFTER SPASMS OF
THE LAST DROPS OF LIFE HAD PASSED
THE MACHINE WAS DONE HE COLLAPSED
DEAD WHERE HIS BODY ROLLED FOUND
BONES AND RAGS IN A DITCH NOT TO FAR
FROM APPERATUS YELLOW DUST HIDING
ITS VICTIMS IN THE WIND FROM SIGHT

GLASS TONGUE

ELIMINATE FROM THIS
THROAT THE GLASS THAT
WAS SWALLOWED AT BIRTH
TORTURING FLESH OF TONGUE
TOXIC LOVE KISS OF THORNS
VENOM VINES TANGLE THE MIND
HANGING FRUIT THE TREE OF TIME
WANTING TO DRAW LIFE BLOOD
WAITING TO ABSORB TEARDROP
EVERYTHING THAT WAS SO CLOSE
WAS REALLY SO FAR AWAY
WITH DAMAGED THROAT
THE TRUTH THAT HURTS
CAN NEVER BE SPOKE

QUARANTINED

WILLOW TREE THAT WEEPS
NEVER DROWNS IN
OCEANS OF SORROW
WIND DAMAGES
WITH WHISPERS
QUIET AND SECLUDED
A TRILLION LARVA
QUARANTINED
IN THE LIGHT OF
LUNAR ECLIPSE
MEMORIES WILL EAT
OF THE TREE
FROM INSIDE OUT
BY THE MORNING STAR
AS BUTTERFLY'S
OPAL MANTRA
WILL SOOTHE
THE HUNGER
WITHIN BY THE FULL
SAPPHIRE MOON

MALIGNANCY

IT MADE ME SICK
ONE DAY I HAD
NO CONTROL
HOW LONG HAD
THE MALIGNANCY
BEEN BURIED
SO MUCH DEEPER THEN
FLESH AND VEIN
NO SURGICAL
PROCEEDURE
FOR ITS REMOVAL
FOR ONE CANNOT
REGURGIATE WHAT
ONE DOES NOT
UNDERSTAND

PAST TENSE

EMPTY FALLING FOREVER
CRYING AS IF LONGING
FOR SOMETHING LOVED
FROM THE PAST
THAT WILL NEVER BE AGAIN
YET THE FLOATING VOID
WAS CALM I WAS AT ONE
WITH SELF AND SADNESS
MY GELATIN WOMB

MEMORY DUST

MEMORIES
FADED FROM MIND
TRACES OF
CHRONOS DUST
ARE LEFT FLOATING
THAT STILL GET
IN MY EYES

EMPTINESS

I CANNOT TASTE YOU
I WANTED TO SEE YOU
TO HOLD YOU CLOSE
BUT I COULD
NOT FEEL YOU
WHY DOES THIS
EMPTINESS
THAT HAS
NO BODY NO MIND
WEIGH SO HEAVY
DEEP INSIDE ME

FORBIDDEN
LOW FEVER

RAGE FEVER
BOILING POINT
PULSING VEINS
HIDDEN UNDER
SKIN ACHING HEART
CANNOT SEE PATH OF
CONCEALED TUMOR
FLESH FLASH FIRE
THESE THOUGHTS ARE
POISON TO MY PAIN
JUST STRANGLED
TUBE SUCKING OXYGEN AIR
FROM BREATH EXHALED
USED WASTED DEPLETED
STILL LIVING OFF
A DEAD LUNG
NON – FUNCTION
ONLY ONE INHALES
THE NEXT BREATH
KNOWING THAT
IT MAY NEVER COME

LETHARGY WASTED

COMA WITH DEAD KISS
A WISH OF WANTING
REALIZING IT WAS NOTHING
BOUND WRIST ANKLE
MARBLE CHUNK COLD
HURTING WARM FLESH
I CAN'T STAND TO
SEE YOUR STARE
HEART MONITOR BEEPING
THE TICK TOCKS OF LIFE
SOUND SLOWING IN
LIQUID COCOON OF DIS – EASE
THE FLESH ONCE BROKEN
CANNOT BE REPAIRED

WRAITH CRIES
IN WAVES

ANGRY TEETH HAS FALLEN
AGED EXHAUSTION
PIN THIS BUTTERFLY
TO THIS SPACE
NO MORE TEARS
THE TIME FOR THAT
WAS OVER YEARS AGO
NON – EMOTION EXISTS
MACHINE FUNCTIONS
AS THE LITHO CELLS
RUN DOWN
ITS PAST TENSE
THE PHASED OUT
CIRCULATION
OXYGEN WAVES
PULLED IN AND OUT
OF THIS NON – EXISTENT
BEACH OF SAND
WHERE NOW ONLY ONE
GRAIN OF SAND IS ALL
THAT REMAINS

DETERIORATE
LIKE MEMORY

MEMORY CIRCUITS
WORN DOWN
GRAPHIC CARD STILL ACTIVE
IN LAYERS OF DUST STORM
RAM AND GHZ PROCESSOR
CONNECTED ETERNAL FRIEND
SECTOR ZERO SUICIDE
SIGNAL IS LOW
ALMOST CRAWLING
DETERIORATION OF
SOLID STATE DRIVE
BIT BY BIT STATIC
SIGNAL GOING DIM
NOT AUDIBLE ONLY NOW
A HUMM OF ECHO
IN A MIRCO MOTHER BOARD
OF BARREN WIRELESS LAND
SUCTION OF DATA
UPLOAD IS UN – COMPLETE
DOWNLOAD HALT
SYSTEM FAILURE
IMMENENT
DEATH OF OS
VERISON OFF

SUFFER THE ISLAND TWIN

ISLANDS OF WASTE
CHAINS OF METAL
JAGGED RUST BLED STAINS
A SKY IS SCARRED GRAYSCALE
STANDS ON THE
LARGEST LAND MASS
SUFFER STARING OUT
UPON FROZEN SMOOTH RIPPPLES
IN AN OCEAN OF CHRONOS ETHOS
ANXIETY FILLED AND LONELY
IT GLANCED DOWN UPON A SPOT
WHERE ITS TWIN NOW DEAD
LAYS IN DE – COMP STATE
THEY WOULD ABSORB EACH OTHERS
PAIN BALANCING IT ALL OUT
TO KEEP LEVELS TOXIC FREE
NOW SUFFER FULL OF FEAR
DOESN'T KNOW WHAT TO DO FOR
IT SOON WILL DIE AND FORGET
EVEN WHY IT KILLED ITS ONLY
TWIN IN THE FIRST PLACE

FLESH STOLEN BUT
NOT OBTAINED

BARRIER HELD WITH HUNGER
NATION ALL BEINGS CONSUMED
IT WAS ALL THEY KNEW
CONSUME SUSTENANCE
CONSUME PHARMA SENSATION
THOUGHT FEELING EMOTION
BUT SOON CHRONOS SHIFTED
TO SHOCK A SPACE FROZEN
CAUSED ANOMALY THEN
ELEMENTS OF CONSUMING
SLOWED TO CATERPILLAR PACE
ONE BY ONE SLOWLY CAME
THE HUNGER VIRUS INFECTION
CALM AT FIRST AS CHRONOS
STRUGGLED A FURY OF PANGS
EATING EMPTINESS FROM
THE IMPLOSION OUT AND THEY
BEGAN A SYSTEM OF CHASING
CANNIBALISTIC ACTION AS THE
FLESH WAS STOLEN NOT OBTAINED
AND MADNESS ENSUED FURTHER

PROTECTION
WILL BURN

ON A HILL OF ONE FATE
A CHARRED HEART LIES
BUT ITS WILL WAS NOT
ENOUGH FOR IT LOVED
AND WITHIN THAT LOVE
IT VOWED TO PROTECT
WHAT IT LOVED BUT
FURY FORCE WAS TOO
STRONG ITS LICK OF FIRE
BURNED THE HEART AND
KILLED THE HEART WHERE
NOW UPON THIS SILENT
HILL IS ITS MORGUE PLACE

CREMATORIUM

BLOOD CLOUD
HANGING AS IF FROZEN
CRIMSON FRENZY
THE LAKE IS WHERE
HEARTS ASHES ARE
DISPOSED OF
SILENT SCREAMS
LIQUID GRAPHITE ASH
HOW MANY PAST TENSE
FILL THE MAW OF SPACE
WINDLESS STILL
CRIMSON FRIGHTENED
SLICK SHAKING
A FEVER SHOCK
THAT ALWAYS
REMAINS

HUNGER

THE MIND SKIN STAINED
WITH MY MISTAKES
I MUST RID MYSELF OF IT
TEARING IT OFF IN PIECES
SINK MY TEETH
INTO ITS TOUGH
RUBBERY TEXTURE
TO CHEW AND RIP IT
IT GETS CAUGHT
IN BITS IN MY THROAT
I SWALLOW THEM DOWN
WITH HELP OF
LIQUID TEARS FROM
BUILT UP PAIN
I AM FULL I KEEP EATING
BUT I NEVER STAY FULL
AND STILL I CHEW AND
KEEP CHEWING…

TEARS OF
THE POPPY

DROWNING IN
DREAM STATE
LUCID TWINIGHT
ENTWINED WITH
BLOOM OF A POPPY
WHEN CUT CRIES TEARS
ARE DEADLY TO ALL
FOR ITS TEARS BRING
NUMB STATE OF
NON – REACTION
A LIVING DEATH WITH
NO CONSCIOUSNESS
WHERE ONE DREAMS
IN DROWNING STATE
WITH THE GHOST
TRAPPED WITH SKIN
NEVER TO DEPART
UNTIL A HEART BEATS
NO MORE

SIGHT OF THE REDEEMER

RAYS BURN DOWN AS IF
ACID UPON TATTERED
TORN GEIST MATTER
OF WALKER INTO AN
UNENDING HORIZON
FOR WALKER SEARCHES
WITH EYES UN – CLOUDED
BY DEFECTS OF SELF THAT
DESTROY THE GEIST'S WILL
KILLING A GREATER LEVEL
OF CONSCIOUSNESS
WALKER PROCEEDS INTO
NERVE ENDINGS HORIZON
TO RISE TOWARDS THE
FUTURE WORLD TO
FEAST UPON ITS OWN
TRANS – FORMATION
FOR ONCE WALKERS
SIGHT IS CLEAR FOR
SIGHT IS THE REDEEMER
TO ONES SELF
REALIZATION

MECHANISM

YOU INSTALLED
MY RAGE AND MY FEAR
CONTROLLING THEM AS
YOU SAW FIT TO WITH
CLOCKWORK PRECISION
NOW YOU ARE GONE
THERE IS NO ONE
TO OPERATE THESE
USELESS BEHAVIOR
PATTERNS OF
DESTRUCTION
OF SELF WITH
DIS – EASE
WHAT WILL
I DO NOW?

THE PAST

I LEFT A PIECE
OF MY HEART IN THE PAST
IT WAS INFECTED
WITH IMPERFECTIONS
I NEVER WANTED IT BACK
IT HURT TOO MUCH
BUT I DID FIND IT AGAIN
WHEN I WENT BACK
TO FIX WHAT WAS BROKEN
IT WAS STILL THERE
COVERED WITH DUST AND
WASTED CHRONOS

CLOCK

A CLOCK ON A WALL
WITH NO HANDS
TIME SEEMS FOREVER
BUT THE CLOCK
DOES HAVE HANDS
WHEN LOOKED AT WITH
A DIFFERENT LENSE
IT HAS HANDS
THEY JUST MOVE
SO FAST NO ONE
CAN SEE THEM

SCREAM WANTED RELEASE

INJECTED RAGE
COULDN'T WHISPER
SLEEP STARVED
FROM DREAMS
YOU COME WHEN
I DON'T CALL
FALLEN FROM A
LONG FLIGHT OF STARS
WILL YOU DREAM
WHEN YOU'RE DEAD
DO YOU SEE IN
MY MIND INFARED
HEAT TRAPPED ME
IN THIS COMA
I SENSE YOU
AROUND WITH ONLY
TWO SENSES
FEAR AND DREAD
TUNNEL VISION
TRAPPED IN
A CUT OPEN VEIN
YOU ARE NOT
REALLY HERE
STAY AWAY
FROM ME

YESTERDAY

SEAS SHIMMER WITH
FLUORESCENT BEAMS
FLOATING IN
3 – DIMENSION
THIS HEART BEATS
IN LULLING WAVES
STARS SINGING IN
THE ATMOSPHERE
OF GAZING HAZE
ABOVE THE WATERS
LAPPING KISS AND
FLOWING TOUCH
OF MANY HANDS
AND FINGERS OF
GHOSTS THAT STILL
SEARCH FOR THEIR
MISSING BODIES
LONG GONE WITH
MEMORIES AND
SIGHS OF YEARS
AND YESTERDAYS

INNER DEATH

FRACTURED BREATH
STRUGGLING TO
BECOME REGULAR
MIND FREEZE FRAME
CAUGHT BURNING IN
LIGHT OF BLIND EYE
SCREAM TRAPPED
IN LUNGS EXHAUSTED
SLEEPWALKING UNTIL
DEAD ZOMBIE STATE
WHEN WILL ELECTRICITY
SPARK TO LIFE IN THIS
BLOOD OF MINE

SOLILOQUY
OF HEART SONG
THE CICADA SPEAKS
INTO THE DUSK…
IS THERE ANOTHER
TO SHARE THIS LIFE?
THE RESONANCE
THAT ANSWERED
WAS A SINGLE
VIBRATION OF ECHO

LOST STAR
THE SORDID UNIVERSE CALLS
YOU YOU DO NOT ANSWER ITS
SANGUINE VOICE
COLD AS THE LONELY BLUE STAR
CONFUSED
LOOKING FOR ANOTHER
IT WAITS…
AND WAITS…
AND WAITS…
AND WAITS…

SYNTHESIS
RUNNING RED
FUSED WITH MY ANXIETY
IT DID NOT LIKE
THIS FEELING WHICH
IT EXPERIENCED
SOMEWHERE
A CRICKET AND SILENCE
BOTH DIED THAT
NIGHT TOGETHER…
THERE WAS NO PHEONIX
NO RESURRECTION
ACCEPT FOR SILENCE
MY ANXIETY FLOATED
UP – OUT AND AWAY
THE RUNNING RED
WAS ALL THAT REMAINED
UNTIL IN THIS MINDS EYE
IT COULD ONLY SEE
THIS RUNNING RED THE SILENCE
STRECTHED AND SWELLED
EVEN THOUGH THE RUNNING RED
COULD NOT FEEL IT ANYMORE
ALL IT FELT WAS
CONSUMED

A LEAF BEGAN TO DIE ONCE
UPON A CHRONOS AGO AND
STARTED TO FLOAT DOWN
TO THE GROUND
HOW COULD THE LEAF FIGHT
FROM FALLING TO THE GROUND?
ANOTHER QUESTION
REMAINS…
HOW CAN ONE
STOP TIME?

RIP AT
YOUR CHEST
AND PULL OUT
THE FEAR
YOU DON'T
NEED IT
ANYMORE

THE SCREAMING LOTUS
HURLED THROUGH SPACE
AT SPEEDS WHICH DISTRACTED
ILLUSION AND CONSCIENCE
THE SANITY FUSING
WITH INSANITY
PHANTOMS REACH INSIDE
THROUGH MY EYES
I FEEL SENSATION
THE BLUE DROWNS MY LUNGS
QUAKING TREMBLES
ZAGGING ALONG THESE
INDIGO SEAS OF ARTERY VEINS
THE METAL VASTNESS
IN VISION EXPANDS
LIKE LIQUID ALKALINE
STRECTHED SKIN OF SOUL
HANGING TAUT FROM
EACH POINT OF STAR
IMPLODED SOUL
EXPLODED SOUL

PANDEMONIUM
PIROUETTES IN TRAILS
OF FIREFLIES LIGHT
PANDORA SAILED NIGHT SKY
ALONG THE SEA OF GALAXY
WISHING BENT SOUND AROUND
QUIXOTIC DREAM
CAN'T WHISPER NO LONGER
SOUND CANNOT
LIVE WITHIN VACUUM
AND BREATHE SILENT
UTTERS OF DISSONANCE
LIQUID OF DELUSION
INVADE MY WEAKENED
AQUALUNG
TIME LEAKED AWAY
INVADE MY WEAKENED
AQUALUNG
TIME LEAKED AWAY
PANDORA SAILED
THE SEVENTH GALAXY
THE KISS THE RAZORS
LIPS SALIVAS TONGUE
TIME LEAKED AWAY

UGLY
CRIPPLED
POISONED GOD
CAN THIS
DAMAGE
BE CURED?

SOFT LIQUID CRY
SPECIMEN OF
VOICES DIED
WASTE ME
TAKE ME INSIDE
WASTE ME INTO
YOUR SCREAM
COCOON ME
WITHIN THE LIMBS
WASTE ME
INTO YOU INTO ME
UNTIL A SLEEP HAZE
DROWNS US
INTO THIS DAZE
SOFT LIQUID CRY

THE STRANGE SUN IS GONE
THE STARS HAVE DIED
NO MORE TO WISH UPON
THEN THERE IS ME
WANDERING IN THIS
DARK GAUZY HAZE
ALL ALONE

TRANSITION OF SOUL
BROKE THE CONNECTION
A SUNSET STREAM
WASTED ITSELF
AND NO ONE SEEN IT HAPPEN
ARTIFICIAL INSEMINATION
COULD NOT EVEN
HAVE BROUGHT IT BACK
TO ITS ALREADY
USELESS LIFE

FROM THE MUTE VISION
THAT SCORCHES
THE WALLS OF CORONA
EMPTY ISOLATION APPEARED
IT WAS NOT FAR
IT WAS NOT CLOSE
BUT I CALLED AND CAME IT DID
IT WAS EMPTY
IT ALWAYS COMES WHEN I CALL IT
IT NEEDS ME
SOMETIMES WHETHER OR NOT
I NEED IT
STILL NEVER FAR
STILL NEVER CLOSE
IT NEEDS ME
I NEED IT TOO

INJECTOR
OF ORGY
THE HUMAN FLESH BODY
SHIVERED
IN ORGASMIC TITILLATION
PRECEPTION WAS
TO ACHIEVE TOTAL RESPONSE
EVEN THOUGH
INJECTOR
PREFERRED
ISOLATION OF
QUASI – MASTURBATION

WEAVE MOIST SKIN
INTO GELATINE LIQUID
DISSOLVE BONE
MELT A PURE HEART
THAT CANNOT BURN
IT WOULD REQUIRE
MORE OF TEMPERATURE
CONTROLLED
METAMORPHOSIS
TO BECOME ENDLESSLY
ANYTHING
DISINTEGRATION
OF THIS THING CALLED
LOVE INTO LOVE
WITH A SINGLE TEAR

UNLOCK
MULTI – POLAR
NEURONS
EYES CONNECT
THE HEART
VEIN MORE BLUE
THAN LIFE BLOOD
SOUND WITHDRAWS
FALLING PLUNGE
YOURSELF INTO
THE SCREAMING WIRES
SHOCK THE
SEA OF BLOOD
THE NERVE
ENDINGS CRY

WAKE THE SHAKES
GROWLING IN THE BIZARRE
DAWN OF UN – BLINKING DREAMS
A CREATURE LIVES THERE
DOWN IN THE VALLEY OF VEIN
THIS WORM WHOSE ENERGIES
SUCK SLOWLY AFTERBIRTH
OF A VERSE OF UNI WOMB
IT RETURNS TO ITS HIVE
SO MANY MATURE EMBRYO
READY TO SWALLOW
READY TO DEVOUR
HOLY EYES
IN ITS CENTER
THE CALALYST

THIN MIND
DIVIDES THE HEART
THRICE ITS LAMENT
MIGRATES
SKIES WEAKEN AND DIE
ONE IS ANXIOUS
INFECTIOUS MATTER
LIKE A VIRUS IN TIME
LIES WAITING
LANGUID DUST INSECTS
FLY THROUGH THE RUINS
OF A DESOLATE CITY
WHERE OBEDIENCE
ONCE LIVED ALONG
WITH DREAMS AND
THE ACOLYTES

CHROME TEETH LIQUID NAILS
LAKE OF RUST THE COLOR
OF MENSTRUAL STREAM
PHANTOM CARRIED THE MUTATION
CLUTCHING IT LIKE CHILD CLOSELY
HE DID NOT KNOW WHAT TO DO
WITH THIS LIVING DEFORMITY
IT WRIGGLED –
IT BREATHED –
IT WRITHED –
STANDING IN THE MIDDLE OF
LAKE OF RUST PHANTOM VOMITS
COPPER BLOOD ONTO IT WHICH
DISGUISES THE MUTATION
HE THEN LAID IT GENTLY INTO THE
RED LAKE WHERE IT WOULD NOT
BE FOUND AND WOULD STAY SAFE
ACROSS THE LAKE
ONE LONE PROTO BIO – MORTAL
SAW WHAT PHANTOM
HAD DONE – CURIOUS?
HE MUST FIND OUT WHAT IT WAS
A VIRTUAL PANDORAS BOX REALIZED
AND PANDORA WAS NO WHERE
TO BE FOUND

I MAKE LOVE
TO MY SECRETS
AT LEAST THEY'RE
SAFE AND CAN'T
HURT ME LIKE
A HUMAN CAN

I DON'T WANT
YOU HERE
KEEP AWAY
FROM FEAR
I DON'T WANT
YOU ANYMORE
DON'T LOOK AT ME
I DON'T WANT
YOUR TOUCH
LEAVE ME ALONE
I NEVER ASKED
FOR YOUR LOVE

MY NUMB HEART
THE THINNER THE AIR
BURNING AT THE STAKE
THIS PIECE OF
FLESH ORGAN
NO SMOKE RISES
FROM THE FIRE
ITS HURT IS NOT
ABSORBED YET
BY THE AIR

BLACK WRAPPED FLESH
FLUID GAUZE COVERED EYES
THEY SEE THE HUNDRED
FORMS OF SLICED SOULS
MISSING PIECES AND PIECES
THROUGH CAUSING CONFUSION
LIKE LOST CHILD THAT
DON'T KNOW WHERE IT IS
PARALYSED FIELD
BURIED SHELLS
OF FORMER BEINGS
THAT CANNOT
BE ANYMORE
WASTE

I LOVED ONCE
A DUST COVERED
MEMORY THAT
FROM ME WAS
ONCE HIDDEN
FULL OF FEAR
LOVE WOULDN'T
RETURN
ITS LOVE TO ME
IT WASN'T
THE FIRST TIME
IT HAPPENED

MOONBEAM TRANSPARENT
CUTTING INTO HAZE OF
YESTERDAYS SHORE
AN OCEAN IN STILLNESS
WAVES ALMOST AT SHORES SAND
IN LIMBO THE SANGUINE SECTOR
PENETRATED THE LIQUID AND
WAITED FOR THE SEMI – HUMAN
TO RISE AS STARS BLINKED
INTO SCENE ONE BY ONE

TEARDROP MEMORY
WANDERS THROUGH
BLACK HOLES HORIZON
FEELING PAST TENSE
BEING PULLED APART FOR
THEY PAINED THIS
FRAIL SALT LIQUID SAC
GRAVITY STRONGER THAN
HEARTBEAT PUMPING VEIN
REFLECTION NOT NEEDED
CAUSING TEARDROP TO
EXIST JUST A SPACE IN
CHRONOS LONGER

SENSATION
AQUIRED ABORTION
REMOVAL IMMENENT
DANGER CAUSED
BLOOD PRESSURE TO RISE
TO ORGAN DAMAGE POINT
BIO – HAZZARD AGENT
USED AN ACID INJECTION
WHICH PURGED SENSATION
FROM SYSTEM CELL
SO CELLULAR MATURITY
COULD COMMENCE

FIRE BURNING AWAY
THE NERVOUS SYSTEM
WHERE ONCE EXISTED
HALLUCINATION
THAT AFFECTED
NEURO FUNCTION
FROM PROPERLY
TAKING AWAY ALL
THE HURT AND PAIN
IT CAUSED NOW NOT
EVEN AN IMAGO
IS LEFT FOR
PARALYSIS STATE
IS NOW THE
END RESULT

I ACHE FOR
THE THINGS
I CANNOT HAVE
EVEN IF THEY'RE
HARMFUL TO ME
I AM NUMB
AT TIMES AND
ITS LONELY

WHY SHOULD
THIS THING CALLED
A HEART WITHIN
THIS STRONG
RIB CAGE BE
SO FRAGILE
SO EASILY
HURT?

IF SCARS
WERE TO HEAL
THERE WOULD BE
NO NEED TO
RE – OPEN
THEM WITH
RAZOR SHARP
MEMORIES

THOUGHT
DOESN'T
HAVE TO
EQUAL
ACTION

MERCURIAL STARS
IMPLODING SOFTLY
MORPHING HUES OF
VACUUM RAINING
RAZOR FRAGMENTS
ONTO THE FLESH
OF HEART UNKNOWN
OF THE TORTURE
IT WAS TO RECEIVE
COLOR BLEEDING
FROM EVERY CUT

SEA SALT DROWNED
LUNGS SPEAKING
IN DREAM WAVES
VIBRATING OFF OF
METEORITE DUST IN
UPPER EXOSPHERE
GHOSTS DREAM OF
MISSING BODIES
PHANTOM PAIN STILL
HURTING INVISIBLE
LIMBS OF SLIPSTREAM
THAT EMBRACE EACH
OTHER AND PIROUETTE
DANCING FOREVER

THE SUN HAS GONE
TO SLEEP AND DREAM
OF YESTERDAYS AND
TOMORROWS
YET HERE I LAY
IN THE EVENING
WITH THESE
SIGHING STARS
AND MY ANIXETY

STARS ABOVE
SHATTER LIKE GLASS
I STARE UP DISTRACTED
BY ITS SHIMMER SPARK
TRYING TO FORGET THE PAST
THEY CUT SLICE INTO MY EYES
BLINDING ME TO THE SPOT
NOW I CANNOT SEE
BUT I STILL REMEMBER
AND NOW I DON'T KNOW
WHERE I AM GOING

BRAIN DEAD
THE METAL RODS
INSERTED INTO
THE TISSUE MATTER
WAVELENGTHS
AWOKEN ELECTRIC
MEMORIES THAT WERE
NUMB FOR SO LONG
ITS FORGOTTEN
HOW TO SPEAK
IT COULD ONLY
HUMM AND CRY FOR
IT COULD FEEL AGAIN
ONCE CHRONOS PASSED
IT WOULD TELL
WHAT HAPPENED TO IT
BUT THAT WAS
ANOTHER
STORY

FEAR RUSHING INTO
THE VEINS OF THIS MOTH
FLOATING IN THE FREEZING
DREAM STATE DRIFTING
FROM STAR TO STAR
WHERE IT FINDS
ONE OF ITS OWN KIND
MISSING ITS ONE WINGS
THE MOTH HELPS THE OTHER
TO PENETRATE THE
EYE NEBULA INTO THE ORB
OF THE WEB DIMENSION
WHERE TOGETHER
THEY WILL BECOME ONE

I KEPT IT FOR
SO MANY YEARS
I HAD TO WAIT
UNTIL MY HEART
WAS READY AS
MY MIND WAS
INTENSE AND
CRUSHED
BUT AT LEAST
I CAN FEEL AND
I AM HUMAN

INDIGO BLOSSOMS
LOOM AMONG THE
WEEPING VESSEL OF
DISINTEGRATION
MIND IS IN JIGSAW

SLEEPWALKING
SUNSET
CONVULSING
IN OZONE
FATAL IN
REVERSE
MY UNREST
DEVOURS
ALL OF THIS
GHOST

MUSIC BY
ANGELO SPIZZARRI

RED HAZE
FUTURESHOCK
SOMNAMBULIST
MELTDOWN
GHOSTLIGHT

ALBUMS AVAILABLE
@ AMAZON, CdBaby
& iTUNES mP3 & CD
facebook.com/
spizzarrimusicofficial
www.SPIZZARRI.com

For more information on
music, books and other
events, please visit
these sites below:

www.SPIZZARRI.com

facebook.com/
spizzarripoetryofficial

instagram.com/spizzarri

twitter.com/spizzarri

"REALITY IS ONES OWN PERCEPTION."

www.SPIZZARRI.com

www.ingramcontent.com/pod-product-compliance
Lightning Source LLC
Chambersburg PA
CBHW060326130626
46553CB00003B/929